•• THE LIBRARY OF FAMOUS WOMEN ••

# MADELEINE ALBRIGHT

## *U.S. Secretary of State*

by
**Rose Blue and
Corinne J. Naden**

BLACKBIRCH PRESS, INC.

WOODBRIDGE, CONNECTICUT

Published by Blackbirch Press, Inc.
260 Amity Road
Woodbridge, CT 06525

**e-mail:** staff@blackbirch.com
**Web site:** www.blackbirch.com

Printed in the United States

10 9 8 7 6 5 4 3 2 1

**Library of Congress Cataloging-in-Publication Data**
Blue, Rose.
Madeleine Albright : U.S. Secretary of State/ by Rose Blue and Corinne J. Naden.
     p.   cm. — (Library of famous women)
   Includes bibliographical references and index.
   Summary: Focuses on the career of the former United States ambassador to the United Nations who became the first woman to serve as Secretary of State.
   ISBN 1-56711-253-6 (lib. bdg. : alk. paper)
   1. Albright, Madeleine Korbel—Juvenile literature. 2. Women cabinet officers—United States—Biography—Juvenile literature. 3. Cabinet officers—United States—Biography—Juvenile literature. 4. United Nations—Officials and employees—Biography—Juvenile literature. 5. Ambassadors—United States—Biography—Juvenile literature. [1. Albright, Madeleine Korbel. 2. Cabinet officers. 3. Ambassadors. 4. Women—Biography.]
I. Naden, Corinne J. II. Title. III. Series.
E840.8.A37B59   1999
327.73'0092—dc21                98-13723
[B]                                 CIP
                                      AC

# Contents

# Introduction

*A great deal of what I did, I did because I wanted to be like my father.*

*— Madeleine Albright*

It is the end of a very long day for Madeleine Korbel Albright, the first woman to hold the job of U.S. secretary of state. She is spending a few moments alone in the kitchen of her Washington, D.C., home. This quiet time is rare. Her day began with an 8:00 A.M. meeting at the White House. From there, she spent two hours with her staff at the State Department, leaving just in time for lunch with the Russian foreign minister. A short plane trip took her to New York City, where she gave a speech at a United Nations dinner. From there, she took a helicopter to the airport and flew home. Now, late at night, she finally rests and spends a few moments alone.

*Opposite page:*
**Madeleine Albright testified before the Senate Foreign Relations Committee in 1997.**

**Madeleine threw out the first pitch for the Baltimore Orioles' 1997 season. She is standing next to Cal Ripken, Jr., who plays third base.**

Madeleine is a combination of charm and wit. She can also be so direct about what she has to say, that some people may feel she is being impolite.

The secretary of state has a distinct sense of personal style. She especially likes hats with big brims, which she wears with great confidence. And she loves gold jewelry. Madeleine is almost never without several gold-link bracelets, which gleam on her left wrist. She even wore them when she threw out the first pitch to start the baseball season for the Baltimore Orioles in 1997!

Madeleine Albright isn't on the go every day—just *most* days. After all, there is much responsibility resting on her shoulders. She is the highest-ranking woman in the U.S. government. As secretary of state, she is the president's chief foreign-affairs adviser. That means she advises the president on political events happening around the world. She is also the top officer in the president's Cabinet.

The Cabinet is made of the heads of the government's major departments. From oldest to newest, they are: State (founded July 27, 1789), Treasury, Defense, Attorney General, Interior, Agriculture, Commerce,

Madeleine arrives in Moscow in 1997. Her duties as secretary of state take her around the world.

Labor, Housing and Urban Development, Transportation, Energy, Education, Health and Human Services, and Veterans Affairs (founded on March 15, 1989). The heads of these departments are chosen by the president of the United States with the consent of the Senate.

As head of the State Department, Madeleine Albright is the sixty-fourth U.S. secretary of state. She was nominated by President William Jefferson (Bill) Clinton on December 5, 1996. Her nomination was approved by everyone who was voting in the Senate, and she was sworn in on January 23, 1997.

**Thomas Jefferson served as the first secretary of state in 1789.**

The duties of the secretary of state haven't really changed much since 1789, when Thomas Jefferson became the first person to hold that position. But they certainly are a lot more complicated. Besides serving as the president's top foreign-affairs adviser, Secretary Albright and her office are responsible for:

- conducting relations with foreign countries;
- granting and issuing passports to U.S. citizens;
- advising the president on appointments of U.S. representatives to foreign countries;
- advising the president on accepting or dismissing representatives of foreign governments;
- participating in international conferences;
- protecting the interests of U.S. citizens in foreign countries;
- overseeing the U.S. Foreign Service.

Of course, the secretary of state also supervises the huge organization that is the Department of State, located on C Street in the nation's capital. It's no wonder that Madeleine Albright has so little free time!

# Chapter 1

# A Wartime Childhood

*My parents were fabulous people who did everything they could for their children and brought us to this amazing country.*

*– Madeleine Albright*

Madeleine Albright has reached one of the highest offices in the U.S. government, but she can never become president of the United States. That's because a U.S. president must be a native-born citizen. Madeleine was born in Prague, Czechoslovakia, on May 15, 1937. She became a U.S. citizen after coming to the United States at the age of 11.

Madeleine's father, Josef Korbel, was from Moravia, which is now part of the Czech Republic. His family moved to Prague, the Czechoslovakian capital, in 1928. It was there that Josef met and eventually married his high-school sweetheart, Mandula Spieglova, whom the family called Anna. Madeleine was their first child. There is some disagreement about

As a young girl, Madeleine moved between Czechoslovakia, Yugoslavia, and England, where she posed for this photograph.

her given name. Most records, however, say that she was named Marie Jana. She was called Madeleine by her grandmother, and her name was legally changed when she was a teenager. The Korbels later had another daughter, Katherine, and a son, John.

## On the Move

Madeleine says that one reason her career has been so successful is that even as a child she often seemed to be in motion. Her father joined Czechoslovakia's foreign service, and represented his country in foreign nations. When Madeleine was still an infant, the family moved to Belgrade, Yugoslavia. Josef worked in the Czech embassy, Czechoslovakia's official offices in Yugoslavia. Between 1937 and 1948, the Korbels moved between Belgrade, London, and Prague. Madeleine claimed that she did not mind. "I made friends easily," she said. She still does.

## The Holocaust Begins

Madeleine may have made many friends during those years, but she was too young to understand the dangers facing her family. When she was born, war clouds were gathering over Europe: World War II was about to begin. Along with thousands of other families, the Korbels would soon be in great danger. Adolf Hitler, the leader of Nazi Germany, had promised that the Nazis would wipe out all of the Jewish people in Europe, as well as other groups, such as the Romani (who were commonly but incorrectly called Gypsies).

*World War II was about to begin. Along with thousands of other families, the Korbels would soon be in great danger.*

The Nazis and their supporters tried to carry out this terrible plan, called the Holocaust, between 1933 and 1945.

After Hitler came to power in January 1933, German Jews were treated with great cruelty. They were removed from jobs in government and education. Jewish-owned businesses were destroyed. Sometimes homes or valuable possessions were taken

A German sign hangs in a city doorway in 1935. It reads, "Jews not wanted!"

from Jewish owners. By 1935, Jews had lost their citizenship. And in late 1938 came *Kristallnacht*, the "night of broken glass." On this night more than 1,000 synagogues were destroyed, along with many Jewish homes and businesses, all across Germany. By 1941, Jews were required to wear a yellow badge with the Jewish Star of David to identify themselves.

There was no great protest in Germany or in other European nations about this treatment of Jews. Most non-Jews decided to pretend nothing was wrong.

But back in late 1938, when Madeleine was barely walking, Hitler was just marching his armies into Prague. By then, the Korbels had returned to Czechoslovakia, and Madeleine's father knew they were in serious danger. Josef Korbel was Jewish, a fact his daughter did not learn until she was an adult. She grew up in the Catholic religion, thinking that the threat to her father was connected with his political beliefs.

## Escape

The Korbels, with their young daughter, fled south in the dark of night to Yugoslavia. That night was the last time any of them saw Madeleine's grandparents.

Adolf Hitler reviews 35,000 Nazi troops that assembled in Berlin, Germany, in 1936.

**Madeleine's parents, Josef and Anna Korbel.**

But Belgrade, Yugoslavia, was no safer than Prague had been. Yugoslavia supported Germany. So, the Korbels escaped the Nazi threat—this time fleeing to Greece. From there, they went to Great Britain, where Madeleine's sister, Katherine, was born in 1942.

During their time in London, when Madeleine learned to speak English, the family moved from place to place. Her father organized radio broadcasts, which were to be sent into Nazi-controlled Czechoslovakia. Reports about mass exterminations began to filter back to England. But no one wanted to believe them.

Years later, when Madeleine became the U.S. secretary of state, a reporter discovered her Jewish background. Madeleine did not seem to know that her parents were raised as Jews. There was immediate criticism directed at her mother and

In October 1997, Madeleine visited Yad Vashem, a Holocaust memorial in Israel.

father, who had changed their religion to the Catholic faith. People wondered why the Korbels, who died in the 1980s, had not told their children about the deaths of Madeleine's grandparents in the Holocaust. Madeleine defended her parents' wishes to keep her from learning a painful truth. But she admitted they probably protected her too much.

## The War Is Over

After World War II ended in 1945, Josef Korbel was appointed to be the Czecho-slovakian ambassador to Yugoslavia. An ambassador is a country's top representative in a foreign nation. Josef took his family back to Belgrade, the city to which they had escaped seven years earlier. In 1947, Madeleine was sent to boarding school in Switzerland, where she learned to speak French. (Today, she speaks English, French, and Czech with ease.) That same year, her brother, John, was born.

By 1948, Madeleine's father was making plans for the family to flee again. For a second time, the family was in danger, this time from the Communists, who were taking over Yugoslavia. (The Communists believed the country should be organized so that all the land and businesses belonged to the government, and the profits were shared by all.) The Korbel family was allowed entry into the United States later that year, settling temporarily in New York City. Early in 1949, Josef learned that the Communists now controlled Czechoslovakia, and they had sentenced him to death.

The Korbels received special protection, called political asylum, from the United States. The U.S. government often helps people who are endangered by the politics of their homeland. The U.S. government gave the Korbels permission to live in America permanently because returning to their native land was dangerous. Starting a brand-new life, they set out for Colorado. Josef was hired by the University of Denver as a professor of international relations (relations between the nations of the world). Young Madeleine, the world traveler, was about to settle down and become an American.

*In 1949, the Korbels began a brand-new life as American citizens.*

# Chapter 2

# A Student with a Sense of Fun

*Madeleine is the image of our father. He set high standards of study, integrity, and discipline.*

*— Katherine Korbel Silva*

Madeleine wanted to become thoroughly American. By the time she finished high school, she spoke English without a trace of a foreign accent. While she was in her teens, she wore Bermuda shorts in summer and a long camel's hair coat in winter. She looked just like any other American teenager of the 1950s.

But Madeleine wasn't really a typical teenager. At a time of life when most young women were interested in clothes or movie stars, Madeleine was already fascinated by politics. And in the heavily Republican area of Denver, Colorado, she was even more unusual. She was a Democrat.

As a youngster and adult, Madeleine greatly admired her father. She rarely went against his wishes. But she does remember one heated disagreement— which she lost. She wanted to attend a large public high school in the city of Denver. Her father wanted her to go to Kent School for Girls, a small private high school in the suburbs. (It is now a school for boys and girls called the Kent Denver School.) Kent offered her a scholarship, and Madeleine went there. Some years later, she admitted to a reporter that "the school did give me a tremendous education."

## Looking Back

Madeleine's classmates at Kent remember her as a serious student with a sense of humor. "Even then, she was immersed in [completely involved with] global political thought," one of them said.

One classmate, Stephanie Allen, recalled that Madeleine had a special ability to connect with people. "She was comfortable with anybody she was with and made us comfortable, too. If the Constitution didn't forbid it, Madeleine really could do it—become the president of the United States."

Another Kent grad, Ardeth Daly Donaldson, remembers Madeleine

The Kent School for Girls in the 1950s, when Madeleine attended.

was good company and had a very sharp wit. "Her parents were fun, too, and enthusiastic about becoming Americanized," Ardeth said. "Madeleine was always studying. She was brilliant about international relations. In fact, she came up with this incredible club."

The club was the International Relations Club, of which she was president. But politics and study weren't her only interests. She sang with the Glee Club and played hockey, too. Stephanie Allen says Madeleine was a "good hockey player."

**Madeleine, seated in the middle, was president of the International Relations Club at Kent.**

Madeleine enjoys thinking about her days at Kent. But she knows her social life could have been better. Her father, schooled in old-fashioned European ways, was strict about dating. "Believe it or not," she once said, "my father used to follow me on dates. He would let the poor boy drive to the dance [and] follow us.... To this day, I will never forget [my] embarrassment when he made me get into his car while my date followed me home."

Madeleine graduated from Kent in 1955. Under her picture, her yearbook stated, "You will often find her taking a definite stand on matters, staunchly saying, 'You guys, this just proves it!'"

In the spring of 1997, Madeleine Albright returned to the Kent School as the nation's first woman secretary of state. She was asked, among other things, what it was like to deal with powerful men who were certainly not used to having a woman in such a high-ranking position.

"You're not going to believe this," she replied, "but I really believe that it is an advantage to be a woman. On my first trip, relations between France and the United States were a little rocky. It helps when the French foreign minister can send me pink roses.... I obviously am

Madeleine's high school yearbook photo, taken in 1955.

In 1997, Madeleine, center, reunited with former Kent classmates. *From left to right:* Julika Balagity Ambrose, Stephanie Allen, Kyle Hicks Reno, and Ardeth Daly Donaldson.

very glad I am the first woman secretary of state, but beyond that, I am very glad there *is* a woman secretary of state." Madeleine added that the United States is a world leader. When a woman is chosen for a responsible position in the U.S. government, the world notices.

During that 1997 return visit to Kent, Madeleine was addressing a group of students when one boy raised his hand. He asked how, as a woman, she got to be secretary of state. She laughed and said,

"Well, if you boys studied harder, you could get to be secretary of state, too!"

One of Madeleine's history teachers at Kent said she was not at all surprised by Albright's success. "Her brilliance stood out…. With the life she led and her concentration, her success seems natural."

## Wellesley and a Wedding

It also seemed natural when Madeleine won a scholarship to attend one of the best colleges in the country. In 1955, she entered Wellesley College, in Massachusetts, to study her two chief passions—politics and journalism, which is news reporting.

Madeleine graduated from Wellesley College with honors in 1959.

Although she would later abandon her journalistic dreams, it wasn't long before Madeleine was involved with politics at Wellesley. She campaigned for Democratic presidential candidate Adlai Stevenson when he ran—unsuccessfully—against Dwight Eisenhower.

Madeleine's classmate Emily McFarquhar said, "The Eisenhower era was a very conservative time. We were among the very few Democrats at Wellesley who campaigned for Stevenson in 1956."

Madeleine graduated from Wellesley with honors in 1959, earning a degree in political science. One of the speakers at her graduation ceremony told the young grads that their main responsibility was to mother a new generation of educated adults. This was the kind of discouraging message that women received in the 1950s, even when they wanted careers.

Three days after graduation, Madeleine got married. The groom was Joseph Albright, a son of a family that owned many newspapers, including the *Denver Post.* They had met two years earlier when both held summer jobs at the *Post.* (It was an odd coincidence that Joseph had the same first name as Madeleine's father, though spelled differently.)

Soon after their wedding, the Albrights moved to Chicago, where Joseph began to work as a reporter for another newspaper, the *Sun-Times.* Madeleine gave up her journalistic career when an editor at the *Sun-Times* said that because her husband worked there, they wouldn't hire her. And neither would any other local newspaper. Madeleine said of that disappointment, "Well, I would have been a lousy reporter anyway."

For a time, she worked for the *Encyclopaedia Britannica* instead. Her dreams of a career no longer seemed so bright.

# Chapter 3

# Washington's Rising Star

*It used to be that the only way a woman could make her foreign policy views felt was by marrying a diplomat and then pouring tea on* [an offensive] *ambassador's lap.*

*– Madeleine Albright*

Just what is a hard-working, brilliant, and outspoken woman to do when she wants a career in politics, and no one is paying attention?  How does she go about having it all—a career and a family?  It isn't easy.

In 1961, the Albrights moved to Long Island, New York, where Joseph worked for a daily newspaper called *Newsday*.  That year, Madeleine gave birth to twin daughters, Anne and Alice.  A third daughter, Katherine, was born six years later.  The Albrights had a housekeeper to help care for their children.  While the girls were young, Madeleine enrolled in the graduate program in Public Law and Government at Columbia University.

She earned a master's degree in 1968, along with a certificate in Russian Studies.

### Foreign Affairs

That same year, the Albrights moved to Washington, D.C. Joseph had been transferred to *Newsday*'s capital bureau. Although the move was made for Joseph's job, it proved to be good for Madeleine's career as well. In 1972, she became involved in Washington politics by helping to raise money for Maine Senator Edmund Muskie, a family friend. Muskie was trying to become the Democratic candidate for president. Muskie was on the Senate Foreign Relations Committee, which deals with relations between the United States and other countries. Madeleine was therefore able to get involved with one of her great passions— foreign affairs. Muskie was not chosen as the Democratic candidate, however, so he stayed in the Senate.

In 1976, Muskie made Madeleine his chief legislative assistant. She was in charge of much of the daily operation of Muskie's office. By that time she had earned a doctorate degree from Columbia University. Now Muskie could introduce her as "Doctor Albright."

*Slowly, word got around that Madeleine Albright was a bright person of growing influence in Washington.*

In the 1970s, Madeleine worked for Maine Senator Edmund Muskie.

    Senator Muskie had a reputation for being a difficult man to get along with, but Madeleine worked well with him. She went about her duties quietly, learning the art of diplomacy (conducting relations between people or foreign nations). She made people feel comfortable and relaxed with her, offering her views in a pleasant manner, but making sure she was heard. Slowly, word got around that Madeleine Albright was a bright person of growing influence in Washington.

## At the Carter White House

When Jimmy Carter became president of the United States (1977– 1981), he chose Senator Muskie to be his secretary of state. He selected Zbigniew Brzezinski as his national security adviser. As luck would have it, when Madeleine was working on her doctorate degree at Columbia University, Brzezinski was her academic adviser. His reputation for toughness was even greater than Muskie's. It was while working with Brzezinski that Madeleine learned she had better be extra well prepared in order to be noticed among all the men with whom she went to school.

Brzezinski had noticed her and didn't forget. He called Albright to work as one of the president's congressional liaisons (go-betweens) with a focus on foreign policy. Foreign policy is a nation's plan for how it will relate to other countries. As a congressional liaison, Madeleine

**President Jimmy Carter**

helped with communications between the president and the Senate. It was a low-level job, but Madeleine made the most of it. A top White House official said, "She was always at the center of things." Brzezinski remembered about Madeleine, "She kept me from getting in trouble with Congress."

Madeleine calmed members of Congress who wanted to do battle with President Carter. She also began to assert her views

Madeleine shares a laugh with Zbigniew Brzezinski and Henry Kissinger at the Gerald Ford Presidential Library.

on most matters that were brought to Carter's attention, such as the nation's troubling relations with China.

Madeleine's position gave her a lot of good experience in foreign policy. But, in January 1981, Jimmy Carter lost his own job to Ronald Reagan, the Republican who had won the 1980 presidential election. That meant Madeleine was out of work, too. It looked as if Madeleine Albright's star was falling. At this point, she left government service.

## Leaving Government

Madeleine decided to become a scholar in Soviet and Eastern European Affairs at the Center for Strategic and International Studies, in Washington, D.C. While she was there, she did research for her book, *Poland: The Role of the Press in Political Change.* It eventually won an award from the Smithsonian Institution's Woodrow Wilson's Center for Scholars. In 1982, Georgetown University's School of Foreign Service appointed her to two positions: research professor of international affairs and director of the Women in Foreign Service Program. Albright remained connected to Georgetown until 1993. During that period of time, she won four Teacher of the Year awards. Her students loved her, according to the school's dean, Peter Krogh. "She was like a pied piper," he said.

Madeleine's career was picking up speed again, but her marriage wasn't. One day in 1982, Joseph Albright came home to tell his wife that their marriage was over. He was in love with someone else. They divorced after 23 years of marriage. Madeleine was sad and upset. She had assumed that she and her husband would always be together, just as her parents were. After the bitterness and anger wore off a bit, Madeleine got on with her life.

## Back in the Swing

Madeleine got back into politics in 1984. She was a foreign policy adviser to the Democratic candidate for president, Minnesota Senator Walter Mondale, and his running mate, Geraldine Ferraro. (Ferraro was the first woman to run for election as vice-president.) Mondale had been vice-president himself when Jimmy Carter was in office.

Mondale and Ferraro lost the election, but Madeleine continued building her career. She turned her home into an

*Madeleine's new position gave her friend Senator Muskie an interesting idea. He thought Madeleine should become secretary of state one day.*

informal center for Democratic foreign-policy makers, who were preparing for the time when they would be back in the White House.

In 1987, Madeleine was on the campaign wagon again as senior foreign policy adviser for the Democratic presidential candidate, Michael Dukakis. During the election, Madeleine wrote many of his speeches and gained a reputation as a person to turn to for advice on foreign policy matters. Her influence among government people was growing stronger, even though, once again, the Democratic presidential candidate lost the election.

**Democrat Bill Clinton won the presidential election in 1992.**

Madeleine's career received an even bigger boost in 1989, when she became president of the Center for National Policy, a Democratic research institute. Madeleine's new position gave her friend Senator Muskie an interesting idea. He thought Madeleine should become secretary of state one day. "She has the ability," he said. "She is as credible, as on top of emerging [new] foreign policy, as anyone I know."

During the many gatherings that took place at Madeleine's home in Washington during those years, hundreds of Democratic leaders and future leaders came to talk and exchange views. Among them was a young, little-known governor from the state of Arkansas. His name was Bill Clinton. In 1992, he decided to run for the presidency.

That year, Madeleine helped to form the Democratic party's political platform— the ideas they wanted to present to the American people during the election. After Clinton won the Democratic nomination for president, she advised him on foreign policy during his campaign.

Clinton defeated Republican George Bush in the presidential election of 1992. After 12 years, a Democrat was finally in office again, and he was ready to appoint a brand-new staff to the most powerful positions in the U.S. government.

# Chapter 4

# U.N. Ambassador

*Yes, it costs money to help keep peace around the world. But by any measure, the most expensive peacekeeping mission is a bargain compared to the least expensive war.*

*– Madeleine Albright*

Bill Clinton announced Madeleine Albright's appointment as ambassador to the United Nations (U.N.) at a press conference in December 1992. The Senate approved the nomination the next month, making Madeleine the second woman to hold that job. The first was Jeane J. Kirkpatrick, who was appointed U.N. ambassador by President Ronald Reagan in 1981.

Clinton's choice for the position shouldn't have surprised anyone. By then Albright was well known all around Washington as a person of influence and ability.

When Albright's appointment to the United Nations was approved by the

In 1993, Madeleine Albright became the second woman to be appointed
U.N. ambassador.

**Madeleine presents her credentials to the U.N. Secretary-General Boutros Boutros-Ghali.**

Senate in January 1993, she conveyed her pleasure to the public. "As a result of the generous spirit of the American people," she proclaimed, "our family had the privilege of growing up as free Americans. You can therefore understand how proud I will be to sit at the United Nations behind the name plate that says 'United States of America.'"

Newspaper columnist Mary McGrory called Madeleine "an intellectual…with a heart."

## What Is the United Nations?

Just what did this intellectual do at the United Nations? And what are the functions of that organization?

Based in New York City, the United Nations is an international organization dedicated to keeping world peace. It grew out of a conference that was held in San Francisco in April 1945, at the end of World War II. It was attended by 46 countries that opposed Germany, Italy, and Japan during the war. The United Nations was a special dream of U.S. President Franklin D. Roosevelt, who did not live to see it become a reality. Today, 185 countries are members. The organization employs more than 53,000 people around the world. The United Nations has its own flag—a white and blue map of the world—and its own post office and stamps.

U.N. branches are spread all over the globe. For example, the World Health Organization is in Geneva, Switzerland; the Food and Agriculture Organization is in Rome, Italy; and the International Atomic Energy Agency is in Vienna, Austria. But the main work takes place at the U.N. headquarters in New York. Its two most important parts are the General Assembly and the Security Council.

*When, on February 1, 1993, Ambassador Albright took her U.N. seat, she did so with the rank of Cabinet officer.*

**U.N. headquarters in New York City**

Every member country belongs to the General Assembly, and each member has one vote. The Assembly meets once a year to decide on matters that relate to the general activities of the United Nations. One of the General Assembly's tasks is to appoint a secretary-general, the chief officer of the United Nations.

The Security Council is generally thought of as the most powerful of all the United Nations' divisions.

It has the main responsibility for keeping world peace. The council has 15 members. Ten of them are nonpermanent, meaning they are elected for two-year terms. Five of them are permanent. They are China, France, Russia, the United Kingdom, and the United States. Their votes are very important.

**As president of the Security Council, Madeleine calls a U.N. meeting on Somalia to order in November 1994.**

On any decision that relates to world peace, all five permanent members must vote "yes." If just one says "no," the plan cannot be acted upon.

The United Nations tries to keep peace among nations with words, not guns. But sometimes that doesn't work. More than once, troops have gone to battle under the blue-and-white flag of the United Nations.

In the 1990s, U.N. troops have been sent to keep the peace in the east-African nation of Somalia, the Caribbean republic of Haiti, the Middle Eastern nation of Kuwait, and in other parts of the world.

Some people think the United Nations is not effective. They say it spends too much money for the little it does. It doesn't seem strong enough to stop a war if the countries involved want to fight. Critics say that the power of the permanent members makes voting meaningless.

But others say that if people are talking, at least they're not fighting. They agree with Madeleine that "any peacekeeping mission is a bargain."

## The Role of the U.S. Ambassador

When, on February 1, 1993, Ambassador Albright took her U.N. seat, she did so with the rank of Cabinet officer.

That hadn't happened since Jeane Kirk-patrick's appointment in 1981. President George Bush had taken away the position's Cabinet rank when he named his U.N. ambassador in 1989.

As U.N. ambassador, Madeleine was a key adviser to President Clinton on foreign policy, and she traveled between Washington, D.C., and New York City about five times a week. The airline staff got to know her well. Frequent trips to

**Madeleine meets with U.N. Secretary-General Kofi Annan in January 1997.**

Washington were just the beginning of her travels, though. During her years at the United Nations, Madeleine inspected peacekeeping operations in at least a dozen countries overseas.

Madeleine has been praised for her work at the United Nations. She handled herself well in an organization where most of the other delegates were men. And she could be tough when necessary. In addition to her regular duties, she spoke out when she thought a government was not protecting women's basic human rights. Madeleine headed the U.S. delegation to the Fourth World Conference on Women in Beijing, China. She also gave speeches on family planning, which is about limiting the number of children in a family.

The United Nations is a huge operation. Madeleine headed a U.S. staff of more than 100. When she wasn't traveling overseas, she was dashing from her office at U.N. headquarters to meetings with the Security Council or with a visiting representative of a foreign country. Every Friday morning was spent with her staff going over the issues of the week.

As in any job she has held, Madeleine tried to get to know the people who worked for her. When she worked at

*During her years at the United Nations, Madeleine inspected peace-keeping operations in at least a dozen countries overseas.*

the United Nations, she gave lunches from time to time for staff members. The lunches were held in an elegant group of rooms at the Waldorf-Astoria Towers. The Waldorf-Astoria has been the official home of the U.S. ambassador to the United Nations for more than 30 years. It offers a spectacular view of the New York City skyline.

The woman who proudly sat behind the sign that said "United States" worked to protect the interests of her country. And she worked to help the United Nations keep world peace. Those goals were high, and they kept the ambassador constantly on the move.

## Chapter 5

# First Woman Secretary of State

*I never dreamed that I could be Secretary of State. Back in Kent, which was a girls' school, we never thought we could be in a position to make decisions for our country.*

*— Madeleine Albright*

Madeleine has developed her own style of working. She sometimes cuddles one of her grandchildren while sorting mail on an important foreign policy issue. She serves cookies to the U.N. Security Council on Valentine's Day. And she is a blunt, no-nonsense talker who doesn't apologize for her opinions.

But in one area, at least, Madeleine is just like all the other secretaries of state who have held the job before her. She doesn't carry a purse. She stopped doing that when she was the U.N. ambassador. "I kept leaving it under a conference table," she said. Now, if she needs a touch of lipstick or a comb for her hair, she just asks one of her staff members to fish it out of his or her pocket. "I don't think the guys much liked to carry my lipstick at first," she once admitted, "but they got used to it." After all, the top-ranking Cabinet member has some extra privileges!

## Madeleine Is Chosen

When Bill Clinton won a second term in the White House in 1996, he needed a new secretary of state. Warren Christopher, who had served during Clinton's first administration, was retiring. Lots of names were suggested for Christopher's replacement, including Madeleine Albright's. Her record at the United Nations was excellent. Another strong candidate was an experienced diplomat, Richard Holbrooke. There were people supporting each candidate. First Lady Hillary Rodham Clinton, another famous Wellesley graduate, was said to favor Madeleine. The two women had met and become friends when Hillary became the First Lady.

Madeleine received a phone call from the president in early December 1996. She thought he had called to offer her the position. Instead, it seemed as if the president just wanted to chat. He asked her about current problems

**President Clinton congratulates Madeleine as she begins her new position as secretary of state on January 23, 1997.**

at the United Nations, and then they hung up. Two days later, he called again. This time he had real news. He was asking Madeleine to become the next secretary of state, and she accepted.

After learning about her mother's new position, Madeleine's daughter Anne said enthusiastically, "She'll show the world a woman can have all the qualities that make a good secretary of state—toughness, aggressiveness, courage—and still be feminine, attractive, and a wonderful mother."

*"I don't shilly-shally [hesitate] much.... I like to get the job done."*

## Setting the Tone

Madeleine began her new position on January 23, 1997. It still amazes her to think she has the same job once held by Thomas Jefferson!

When she met her new staff at the State Department, Madeleine said, "I'm the one you report to. I don't shilly-shally [hesitate] much.... I like to get the job done." But she encouraged her staff to express their opinions, too. "Don't be shy," she told them.

During her first week on the job, Madeleine set a positive tone for the State Department. "The United States must lead," she said. By early March, she was on a tour of nine nations, including South Korea and China. Later, she attended a ceremony in Hong Kong when it was transferred from English to Chinese rule.

Madeleine has been criticized for being too quick to bring U.S. troops into trouble spots around the globe. For example, some people were against bringing the U.S. military into the Eastern European nation of Bosnia and Herzegovina in 1997. Madeleine has said that she sees little point in having a strong military if it isn't to be put to use.

Madeleine chooses the course she believes to be the right one. She will go anywhere the trouble and action are—Bosnia, Haiti, or any place that she feels needs her attention.

**Madeleine refused "to tread water" at the 1997 and 1998 peace talks in the Middle East.**

## Working for Peace in the Middle East

One of the most difficult situations Madeleine faced during her White House years was the relationship between the Jewish government of Israel and the Palestinian Arabs who live in that country. The Palestinians refer to it as Palestine. They would like to set up their own government, and they want their own territory. Madeleine worked hard to help the Israeli leader, Benjamin Netanyahu, and the Palestinian head, Yasir Arafat, to reach an agreement. But as she has said herself, she doesn't like "shilly-shallying."

At one meeting she attended with the two leaders, the talks dragged on with little progress. An irritated secretary of state left Jerusalem, saying, "I will come back here when the leaders are ready to make the hard decisions. I will not come back to tread water."

Madeleine and Israeli leader Benjamin Netanyahu held a press conference on the Middle East peace talks in September 1997.

## Trouble with Iraq

In 1997, Madeleine helped Bill Clinton deal with another serious problem in the Middle East, this time in Iraq. The Iraqi president, Saddam Hussein, refused to let U.N. inspection teams search freely for illegal weapons, such as those used in chemical warfare. Hussein wanted to forbid the team from looking in certain places. This, of course, made the member countries of the United Nations very suspicious.

**Madeleine visited with U.S. troops at the Zagreb Airport in Croatia around May 30, 1997.**

When Hussein continued to resist cooperating with the inspection teams, the United States threatened to use force against Iraq. Madeleine spent a lot of time in Europe trying to get the support of U.S. allies in case physical force had to be used.

Madeleine explained the United States' position in an article that she wrote for *Newsweek* magazine. "Why do we care so much about access for weapons inspectors? Because Saddam has a long track record of aggression and deception. Unlike any other modern leader, he has used chemical weapons against other countries and even against his own people."

## More Work at the United Nations

As secretary of state, Madeleine also took on the problem of the United States and its nonpayment of dues to the United Nations. This became a personal crusade. Although all member nations are required to pay dues to the United Nations, for some time the United States has refused to do so. The U.S. debt eventually rose to about $1 billion. The U.S. Congress claimed that the dues were too high and that the United States gave up too much authority to U.N. leadership.

In protest, the Senate Foreign Relations Committee, headed by North Carolina Senator Jesse Helms, had held up payment of this debt.

Madeleine objected. "We need the U.N.," she said, "and the U.N. needs our dues." So, she set about trying to find a compromise. To do so, she developed a close working relationship with Helms. After some negotiations between Congress and the United Nations, the debt was reduced to $800 million. Congress is now nearer to a final resolution of the nation's U.N. debt, thanks to Madeleine.

## Madeleine Albright as Role Model

Many people in the United States are wondering if this hard-working, powerful woman will help others of her sex to reach out for higher goals. Improvement in the lives of women all over the world is certainly one of her most treasured wishes. Does her appointment help to open the door for others?

One student from Yreka, California, thought so. In an online chat on the Internet, she wrote Albright: "I am disappointed that I didn't get to talk to you...maybe another time, when *I* am secretary of state."

Geraldine Ferraro, the first woman to run for vice-president of the United States, said, "The primary reason I was chosen to run for vice-president was to break a barrier. In 1996, Madeleine was chosen because of her expertise. When everyone is judged solely on merit, women do very, very well."

Because she goes wherever the concerns of the United States take her, it would seem that Madeleine Albright has little time for family life. But she adjusts in small ways.

Madeleine and three other members of the Cabinet. *Left to right:* Richard Riley (Education), Donna Shalala (Health and Human Services), and William Daley (Commerce).

**Madeleine with daughters, from left to right, Alice, Anne, and Katherine.**

Her daughter Anne remembers a time when her mother was speaking on the telephone to the secretary-general of the United Nations. She held the phone with one hand while her new grandson was in her other arm. Obviously, having a career-minded mother was not lost on any of the three Albright daughters.

Two are lawyers and the third is a banker. Says Anne, "The one thing she really wanted to teach us was to do your best at your job, no matter what it is."

Madeleine is very close to her daughters and her sister. Her daughter Anne also lives in Washington, D.C., and her sister Kathy, a former school principal, is close by at the Department of Education. "Sometimes I ask her about work," Kathy admits, "and she'll roll her eyes and say 'please.' That means 'give me a break.'"

**As one of the most powerful people in the U.S. government, Madeleine is accustomed to being at the center of attention.**

The secretary does like a little fun now and then. She kept a basketball signed by the Harlem Globetrotters—a New York team that makes fun of professional basketball—on her desk at the United Nations. It was reported that she once did a few polka steps on an airplane flight from California to Washington. Is that true? No one is talking!

Madeleine Albright has much to be proud of. This thoroughly American woman has survived the dangers of being a refugee and the difficulties of starting a new life in a new country. With determination, hard work, and intelligence, she has become the highest-ranking woman in the U.S. government.

Does Madeleine enjoy being at the center of international politics? It would seem so. On one occasion, she and President Clinton arrived in Prague, the capital of the Czech Republic. They were there for a meeting with another former refugee from the Communists, Czech President Vaclav Havel. As she left the airplane and walked toward her old friend, she turned to President Clinton and said with a wide smile, "It doesn't get better than this!"

# Glossary
*Explaining New Words*

**ambassador** The top official who represents his or her government in a foreign nation.

**Communists** A political group that believes all of a country's land, property, and businesses should belong to the government, and the profits should be shared by all.

**democratic** Favoring a democracy, a way of governing in which the people vote for their leaders.

**diplomacy** The art and skill of conducting affairs between people, institutions, or nations.

**diplomat** A person who speaks and acts on behalf of his or her country's government in a foreign country.

**foreign affairs** Matters having to do with international relations.

**foreign policy** A nation's plan for how it will relate to other countries.

**foreign relations** Matters having to do with how countries get along with other countries.

**intellectual** A person who enjoys spending his or her time thinking and learning.

**politics** The discussions and activities having to do with a country's government.

# For Further Reading

Feinberg, Barbara S. *The Cabinet* (Inside Government series). New York: Twenty-First Century Books, 1995.

Freedman, Suzanne. *Madeleine Albright: She Speaks for America* (Book Report Biographies series). Danbury, CT: Franklin Watts, 1998.

Howard, Megan. *Madeleine Albright.* Minneapolis, MN: Lerner Publications, Co., 1998.

Jacobs, William Jay. *Search for Peace: The Story of the United Nations.* New York: Atheneum, 1994.

Maass, Robert. *UN Ambassador: A Behind-the-Scenes Look at Madeleine Albright's World.* New York: Walker & Co., 1995.

Pollard, Michael. *United Nations* (Organizations That Help the World series). New York: Atheneum, 1995.

# Web Sites

For information on Madeleine Albright's travels and speeches, go to:
**http://secretary.state.gov**

For more information on Madeleine Albright, including a biographical statement and a description of her duties as Secretary of State, go to:
**http://secretary.state.gov/www/albright/ index.html**

To find information on the U.S. State Department, including the activities of the Secretary of State, go to:
**http://www.state.gov**

To connect to an educational site and find information on the U.S. State Deparment, U.S. Diplomats, international affairs and issues, and the travels of the Secretary of State, go to:
**http://geography.state.gov/htmls/ plugin.html**

# Index

**Photo Credits:**
Cover, title page, and pages 6, 7, 11, 16, 25, 29, 31, 48, 52, and 56: courtesy of the U.S. State Department; page 4: ©Martin Simon/SABA; page 8: ©National Portrait Gallery; pages 13 and 15: courtesy of USHMM Photo Archives; page 17: ©Ricki Rosen/SABA; pages 21, 22, 23, and 24: courtesy of Kent Denver School; page 30: courtesy of the Jimmy Carter Library; page 34: courtesy of The White House; page 37: ©M. Grant/United Nations; page 38: ©John Isaac/United Nations; page 40: ©Bruce Glassman/Blackbirch Press; pages 41 and 43: ©Evan Schneider/United Nations; page 50: ©Najlah Feanny/ SABA; page 51: ©Matty Stern/United States Information Service; page 55: Haviv/SABA; page 57: ©Patrick J. McDonald/U.S. State Department.